DANGEROUS DRUGS

STEROIDS

DANIEL BENJAMIN

Cavendish
Square

New York

Published in 2014 by Cavendish Square Publishing, LLC
303 Park Avenue South, Suite 1247, New York, NY 10010

Copyright © 2014 by Cavendish Square Publishing, LLC

First Edition

Website: cavendishsq.com

This publication represents the opinions and views of the author based on his or her personal experience, knowledge, and research. The information in this book serves as a general guide only. The author and publisher have used their best efforts in preparing this book and disclaim liability rising directly or indirectly from the use and application of this book.

CPSIA Compliance Information: Batch #WS13CSQ

All websites were available and accurate when this book was sent to press.

LIBRARY OF CONGRESS CATALOGING-IN-PUBLICATION DATA
Benjamin, Daniel.
Steroids / Daniel Benjamin.
p. cm. — (Dangerous drugs)
Summary: "Provides comprehensive information on the dangers of steroid abuse"
—Provided by publisher.
Includes bibliographical references and index.
ISBN 978-1-60870-826-0 (hardcover) ISBN 978-1-62712-062-3 (paperback)
ISBN 978-1-60870-832-1 (ebook)
1. Anabolic steroids—Juvenile literature. I. Title.
RC1230.B46 2013
362.29'9—dc23
2011037908

EDITOR: Christine Florie   ART DIRECTOR: Anahid Hamparian   SERIES DESIGNER: Kristen Branch

EXPERT READER: Dr. Peter Carek, Residing Program Director, Medical University of South Carolina, Charleston, South Carolina

Photo research by Marybeth Kavanagh

Cover photo by Bob Jones/Alamy

The photographs in this book are used by permission and through the courtesy of: *Alamy*: Bob Jones, 1; Alex Ardenti, 7; PCN Photography, 9; Corbis Flirt, 12; Nucleus Medical Art, Inc., 25; tdbp, 43; ITAR-TASS Photo Agency, 54; *Phototake*: Steve Oh, M.S., 4; Medicimage, 33; *The Image Works*: Sven Simon/ullstein bild, 11; *Newscom*: Custom Medical Stock Photo, 13; Carrie Devorah/Wenn Photos, 28; Arnold Gold/New Haven Register/ZUMA Press, 50; *AP Photo*: Kent Homer, 14; *age fotostock*: Dennis MacDonald, 20; Joseph Sohm/Visions of America, 37; Massimo Dallaglio/TIPS Images, 56; *Photo Researchers, Inc.*: Dr. P. Marazzi, 24; Cosmocyte, 27; *SuperStock*: imagebroker.net, 35. Most subjects in these photos are models.

Printed in the United States of America

CONTENTS

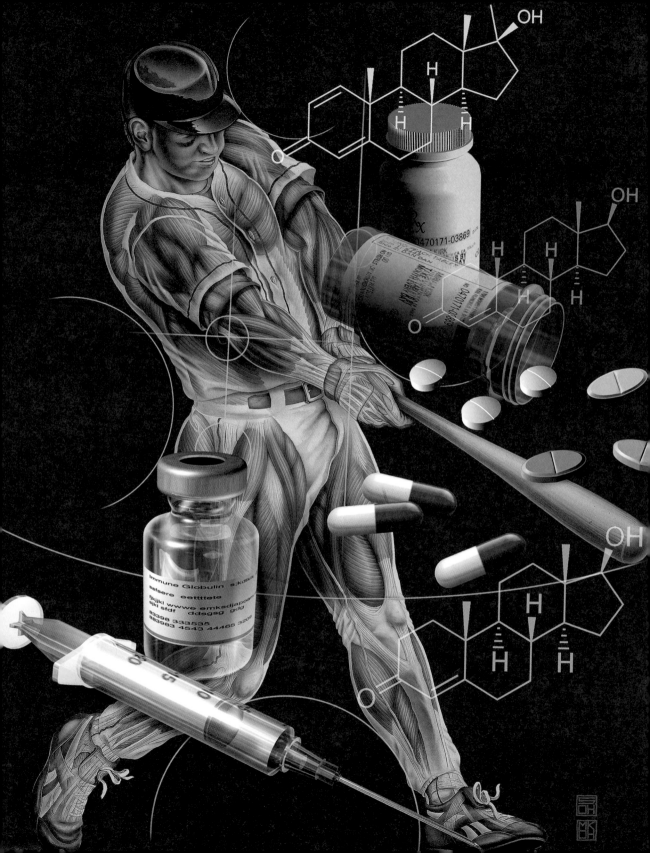

CHAPTER ONE

What Are Steroids?

AROUND THE GYM THEY ARE CALLED *juice, pumpers, stackers,* or *gym candy*. In a chemist's laboratory, they are called **anabolic steroids** or just plain steroids. For decades athletes have been using these performance-enhancing drugs to give themselves an unfair advantage in their sports. Today, even people who are not sports fans have heard of the "'roid" scandals involving athletic heroes such as Olympic biker Lance Armstrong and baseball player Barry Bonds, both of whom stand accused of using illegal drugs to elevate them above their competition.

Left: From major league athletics to high school sports, anabolic steroids lure with the promise of speed, strength, and having an "edge." However, there is great risk in using them.

5

But what are steroids, and how do they work? Put simply, steroids are drugs that attempt to have the same effects as **testosterone**, a hormone that helps build muscle and bone mass. First identified in the 1930s, anabolic steroids are prescribed by doctors for hormone deficiency in males and muscle loss associated with certain medical conditions such as Acquired Immune Deficiency Syndrome, or AIDS. Like any powerful drug, steroids come with a long list of harmful side effects—but when monitored by a responsible doctor, some patients can greatly benefit. One of the most often prescribed is prednisone, a steroid used in the treatment of many kinds of arthritis and some cancers.

Unfortunately, most steroid use today is steroid abuse, which amounts to large and frequent injections of testosterone or similar drugs taken by people who want to improve their performance on a sports field or just look better. Taken in large doses and coupled with intense weight lifting regimens, steroids help the user gain weight and build larger muscles, often in a matter of weeks. Unfortunately, for every pound gained and every muscle bulked up comes a long list of harmful side effects. Steroid users often suffer from severe acne, liver damage, reduced sex drives, heart disease, and a host of other health problems.

People who lift weights while taking steroids experience weight gain and muscle growth in a relatively short period of time. However, acne, liver damage, and behavioral problems can occur as well.

So if you're feeling that you want to get a little bit faster or a little bit stronger, be careful. A good diet and regular workouts are your most healthy, safe bet. Playing with steroids is playing with poison. Yes, you might get bigger muscles in the short term, but the long term costs to your health could be disastrous and, in some cases, deadly.

American Kids on Steroids

For years now, steroid abuse in the United States has been the dirty secret that most high school coaches have been unwilling to discuss. Today, studies suggest that upwards of one million kids, have experimented with steroids. And these numbers do not even include the hundreds of children who have unknowingly taken steroids in spiked dietary **athletic supplements** available at local health food stores. Contrary to what some people might think, steroid abuse is widespread with girls as well as boys. Approximately 6.8 percent of U.S. teenage males have tried performance-enhancing drugs, and 5.3 percent of the girls have also used steroids, either to help them athletically or to just slim down.

Some can be taken orally, in pill form, but anabolic steroids are most effective when injected. Unfortunately, there are many teenagers who are willing to stick a needle,

Some athletes are willing to subject their bodies to the effects of steroids in order to be the strongest or fastest in their sport.

often in their rear ends (or to have a friend do it), to bulk up. After all, successful student athletes are the stars of their schools. Some teens will use any advantage to be the captain of the football team or the ace pitcher in baseball. Add to that the pressure for scholarships. With college costs increasingly on the rise, some steroid users see sports as their only ticket to a higher education. Steroids won't make a user more agile or coordinated, but they do add strength and muscle, enabling the user to better pound a baseball out of a park or hurl a lacrosse ball at the goal. Who would want to stop taking a drug that lets athletes throw harder and run faster?

The answer should be you or anyone else you know with a sense of fair play or even a passing concern for his or her own health. With steroids, an average athlete may bulk up to win a big game. But in the long run, steroid users are big losers.

STEROIDS FOR SELF-IMAGE

Adolescence is a painful time, a period of life when most people feel awkward about their rapidly changing body. An occasional teenager might grow up tall and muscular. But most teens either feel too skinny, too fat, too short, or too weak. Most feel too ugly. Boys and girls can be horribly jealous of skinnier, stronger, taller classmates. Why not take steroids? Why not "even" the playing field? As one teenager put it, "Why not add on what God forgot?" These so-called mirror athletes aren't on teams but take steroids to look better and improve their self-esteem. Although muscles might have a short-term positive effect on one's self-image, the long-term effects of the drugs can be disastrous.

Teenage steroid users who haven't reached their full height risk damaging their bones and stunting their growth. The teen steroid user who takes the drug to be bigger and taller might well make himself permanently shorter!

In 1954 the Russian weight lifting team exploded out of nowhere to dominate the Summer Olympics, winning medals in every category. The story goes that John Zeigler, a doctor who worked with the U.S. weight lifters, asked a Russian physicist what drugs his lifters were being given. The answer: testosterone. Rumors of discarded syringes in the Russian locker room were further evidence that a new and powerful drug had hit elite sports.

STEROIDS IN THE OLYMPICS

By 1958 Dr. Zeigler had developed methandrostenolone, an anabolic steroid with more limited side effects. In the 1960s steroid abuse became common in Olympic and many professional sports. In 1988 Olympic sprinter Ben Johnson (above, far right) broke the world record in the 100-meter dash, only to have his medal stripped when he tested positive for steroid use. But he wasn't alone. In 2003 evidence was leaked to *Sports Illustrated* magazine that showed more than one hundred athletes had failed drug tests but had been allowed to compete in the Olympics anyway.

Today, the use of anabolic steroids is banned by every major sporting body in the world. But today's athletes and trainers have become experts at masking the drugs in urine and blood tests, thereby disguising steroid use. Until a consistent and fair way to test all athletes for steroids is developed, the powerful drugs will continue to be abused.

Many teens are unhappy with how they look and take steroids to improve their physique.

Like any drug, after a user starts, it's very hard to quit. A single cycle of steroids might add muscle to a person's physique. But to maintain those new muscles and make them even larger, the user has to take more and more drugs. The dose of steroids taken by most athletes is horribly high by conventional medical standards. Many athletes "stack" different steroids on top of each other, taking upward of one hundred times the amount of drug needed to produce a normal testosterone level. Along with "stacking," athletes "pyramid" the drugs, taking larger and larger doses over a period of weeks, then gradually decreasing them. When their body recovers from the influx of testosterone, they start another cycle, often stacking doses and pyramiding at the same time. Of course, like any drug, the more you take, the worse the side effects. And it is very rare for a steroid user who mixes these powerful

12

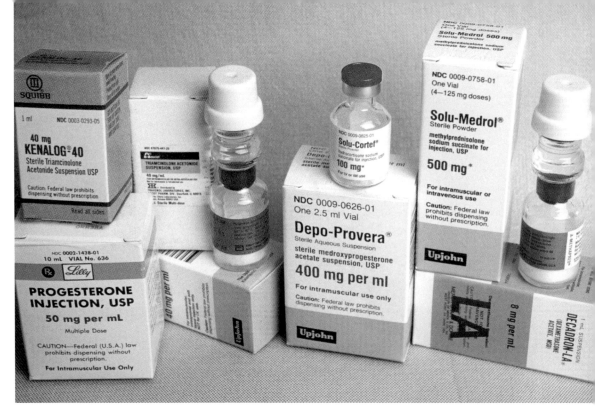

In order to achieve and maintain muscle growth, some athletes "stack" steroids, taking much larger doses than is considered safe.

medications to do so under the guidance of a doctor, making the whole adventure that much riskier.

So the next time you look in the mirror and you aren't happy with what you see, remember this: no teenager since the dawn of time has looked in the mirror and been entirely happy with what he or she has seen. Feeling awkward is part of growing up. The way to combat it is to be aware that adolescence is a passing phase. Get involved with activities you like. Hang out with supportive friends. Before you know it, you will have grown naturally into your body.

THE JUICED ERA OF BASEBALL

In 1994 Major League Baseball lost the end of its season to a strike. When play resumed, angry fans stayed away from ballparks in droves for years. Enter Mark McGwire of the St. Louis Cardinals and Sammy Sosa (below) of the Chicago Cubs. In 1998 these two sluggers went on a hitting tear, swatting seventy and sixty-six homers, respectively, breaking Roger Maris's season home run record of sixty-one. The fans loved it, and ballparks were filled. By that point, it was already a dirty secret that some of baseball's biggest sluggers were on performance-enhancing drugs. Then in 2001 Barry Bonds hit a walloping seventy-three homers. Later, McGwire, Sosa, and Bonds were all accused of using steroids, along with other famous ballplayers such as pitcher Roger Clemens. In 2005 Major League Baseball implemented a stricter policy on steroid use that includes random testing and a fifty-game suspension for first-time offenders.

Steroids: Easy to Get and Many to Choose From

Today, the use of steroids is a federal offense, punishable by fines and prison time. But when searching the Internet, one would never know it. One reason that steroid use is so high is that the drugs are easy to get. The Internet is filled with websites full of false or misleading information that encourage steroid abuse. Teenagers with access to a credit card can order drugs online. Adolescents in Texas, California, or other Southwestern states can make a quick trip down to Mexico where steroids are legal and some pharmacies even have a doctor on hand to inject the drugs on the spot. Worst of all, some coaches supply their players with steroids or at least look the other way when confronted with obvious steroid abuse.

Steroids have come a long way since 1958 when John Zeigler developed methandrostenolone for U.S. weight lifters. Additional drugs such as Malogen, Delatestryl, Anavar, Android, and Ora-Testryl comprise a short list of the many different steroids available to be taken either alone or in combination. Today's steroid user is like a kid in a candy shop: there is so much to choose from, and everything looks good.

CHAPTER TWO

Steroid Side Effects

HAVE YOU EVER BEEN CHANGING FOR gym in the locker room and heard a serious student athlete say something like this?

> "Oh, come on! How can a drug that makes me so
>   much stronger be bad for me?"
> "Who cares if I break out a bit? A few zits are
>   worth making the starting line."
> "I've got this under control. I'm too smart to use
>   too much!"

Even if you haven't heard a friend or classmate make that kind of excuse, you can be sure that someone is thinking it. Despite all the negative publicity about steroids over

the past few decades, many teenagers refuse to see the health risks. Sure, it's too bad that Mark McGwire was forced to admit to using Andro, a steroid-laced supplement, when he bashed seventy homers. But the drug worked, right? His only problem was getting caught. Guess again. The list of health problems associated with steroid use is long, real, and extremely dangerous.

Anyone who thinks he can take steroids and escape the side effects is fooling himself. Bottom line: the new muscles come from pumping massive amounts of testosterone into one's body. All that extra testosterone harms practically every internal organ. What follows is a description of some of the most commonly found side effects of steroid use and their causes.

Injuries

True, many steroid users develop gigantic muscles. But the tendons and ligaments that support those muscles don't grow along with them. This is why many steroid users, including many famous athletes, become injury prone while using performance-enhancing drugs. Tendons rip; cartilage tears; hamstrings pull—all in the name of trying to support a massive influx of new, powerful muscle.

SIDE EFFECTS

What follows is a short list of some of the most common side effects of steroid use:

FOR EVERYONE

- Bones stop growing
- High blood pressure
- High cholesterol
- Blood-clotting disorders
- Hair loss
- Severe acne, often on the back
- Oily skin
- Puffy cheeks
- Liver cysts leading to possible liver cancer
- Increased chance of injuries to joints and tendons
- Aching joints
- Bad breath
- Aggressive behavior called "'roid rage"
- Feelings of inadequacy

FOR BOYS

- Gynecomastia (growing breasts)
- Testicular atrophy
- Low sperm count
- Impotence/sterility
- Prostate growth
- Cancer
- Premature balding

FOR GIRLS

- Male body hair (e.g., beard)
- Male pattern baldness
- Deepened voice
- Irregular periods
- Breast shrinkage
- Potential birth defects

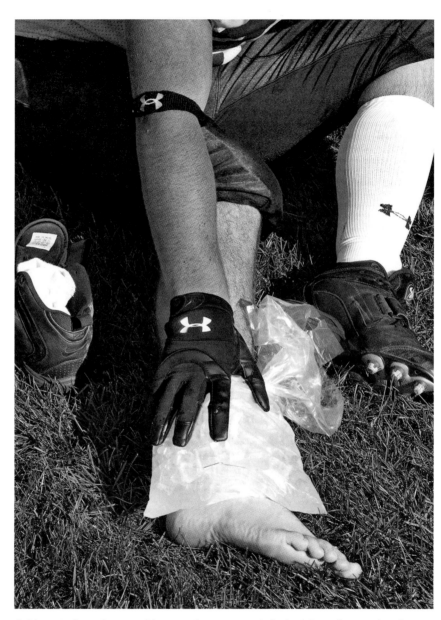

Athletes who take steroids experience more injuries than those who do not.

Look around. Professional sports are filled with massive athletes on the disabled list. All those muscles won't and don't do an athlete any good if he or she is warming the bench with a pulled hamstring or ligament.

Steroids Make You Taller? Guess Again

Boys and girls who haven't finished growing face enormous risks in taking steroids. As a human being matures, **epiphyseal plates** located on the end of certain bones remain open, permitting growth. Then, when adulthood is reached, these plates fuse, ending vertical growth. But too much additional testosterone in a teen's body can cause hormones to send false maturity messages to the bones, resulting in the premature fusion of growth plates and reduction in overall height. In other words, steroid use can briefly speed up a person's growth but then shut it down completely. As a result, teen steroid users often end up being shorter in adulthood than they would have been had they steered clear of performance-enhancing drugs.

Reproductive Troubles

With small doses of anabolic steroids, some men feel increased sexual desire. But with any kind of high dose—

and almost every user requires high doses to build all those muscles—steroids have an opposite effect. What happens is this: large influxes of testosterone make the body think that it is producing too much male hormone. As a result, a male user's testicles shrink.

Though this horrible side effect reverses when the drug is stopped, it happens very slowly. Worse, an unpredictable amount of each dose of anabolic steroids is converted by the body into estradiol, a female sex hormone that can lead to the development of breast tissue in men. That's why it's not all that unusual to see bulked up weight lifters who look like they could use a bra. So before you use steroids, ask yourself: are larger, feminine breasts worth all of those new muscles?

Risks in Needle Sharing

Bottom line: the steroids that work best are the ones that are injected. Steroids taken orally, or in pill form, just don't get the job done—or not nearly as well. That means that a steroid user has to use a needle and syringe. Of course, few, if any, teenagers are trained in how to inject drugs. Poor injecting techniques can lead to a host of problems, including serious bacterial infections and even **gangrene**.

Other side effects include bleeding, bruising of the skin, rupture of tendons, and a variety of allergic reactions. Worst of all, sharing dirty needles can lead to the transmission of Human Immunodeficiency Virus, or HIV, the virus that causes AIDS, and Hepatitis B or C—all serious, and even fatal, diseases.

Acne and Hair Loss

Perhaps the most common sign of steroid use is severe acne, often on a user's back. What happens is this: the sebaceous glands, which secrete oils in the skin, can become excessively stimulated when the body's hormone levels are increased. Elevated testosterone levels lead to oily skin, which often results in severe acne and welts on the back, shoulders, and face. In other words, all those muscles may look pretty, but your skin most certainly won't.

But acne isn't the only way that anabolic steroids can mar your looks. An increase in the body's natural testosterone levels also accelerates male pattern baldness, causing users, both male and female, to lose their hair. The hormone DHT (dihydrotestosterone) is the main culprit. DHT binds to hair follicles on the scalp, causing them to loosen and eventually fall out. This is one of those side

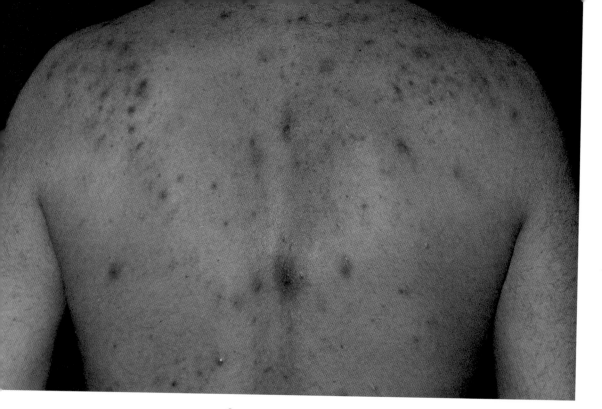

Severe acne on the back is a common side effect of steroid use.

effects that does not reverse itself. Steroid damage to the hairline is permanent. Again, lots of shiny, new muscles might make you feel good about yourself, but being bald most certainly won't.

CARDIOVASCULAR DISEASE

Severe acne and hair loss are upsetting side effects of steroid use. But compared to what 'roids can do to a person's heart, they are relatively harmless. It's one thing to break out or lose hair. But large doses of anabolic steroids can lead to a thickening of the walls of the heart, making it harder for

this all-important muscle to pump blood, a side effect that has been shown to lead to heart attacks. That isn't all that steroids do to a user's **cardiovascular system**. Anabolic steroids decrease the level of so-called HDL (high-density lipoprotein), or good cholesterol, in a person's blood, while increasing the level of LDL (low-density lipoprotein), or so-called bad cholesterol. This can lead to the sort of buildup on artery walls that can result in heart attacks.

Steroids' harm to the heart doesn't stop there. Anabolic steroids add water and salt to a user's body, leading to high

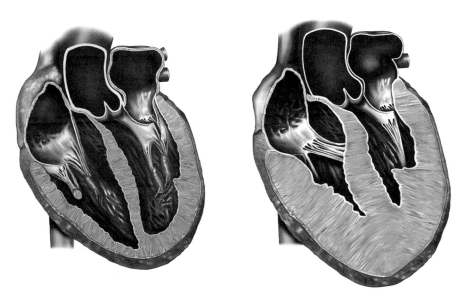

This cutaway graphic illustrates the condition of a normal heart (left) and one with thickened walls, a side effect of large doses of steroids.

blood pressure, which in turn can lead to heart disease, stroke, or kidney failure. On top of that, sudden weight gain stresses a user's heart even more.

Finally, the use of anabolic steroids has been shown to make it harder for the blood to clot. A steroid user will discover that nosebleeds and minor cuts take longer to stop bleeding. Though a stubborn nosebleed isn't anything to worry about, steroid users might run into trouble if undergoing surgery.

So again, think before you shoot up. Steroids might make you look stronger and healthier, but in the process you are putting yourself in danger. A person can live without rippling muscles. But try living without a heart.

Liver Disease

The damage to a person's internal organs from steroid use doesn't end with the heart. Anabolic steroids in pill form can cause a variety of liver diseases. Most often, steroids will cause a benign, or relatively harmless, tumor that might go away when the drug is discontinued. Occasionally, however, these tumors are serious and even fatal. Anabolic steroids also occasionally cause peliosis hepatis, a condition where blood-filled cysts develop on

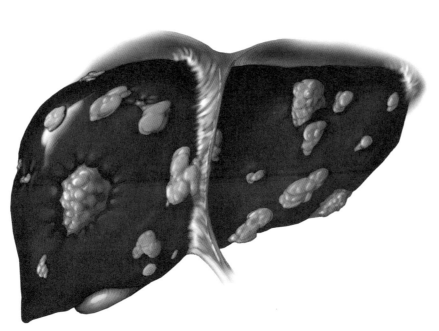

This graphic illustrates a liver that has developed tumors, a serious side effect of anabolic steroid use.

the liver. Often, these cysts can be harmless. But if they burst, they are fatal.

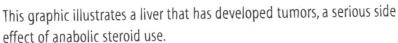

'Roid Rage

Perhaps the most common and, often, the most severe effect associated with steroids is "'roid rage," or overly aggressive behavior. Scientists have found that greatly increased levels of testosterone make lab rats more violent. Scientists have also speculated that anabolic steroids can unmask previously undiagnosed **psychiatric** conditions that were kept in check until the user started to use drugs.

Even so, it's sometimes hard to measure whether a person is being aggressive because of steroids or because it is his or her natural disposition. After all, many steroid users are already highly competitive, aggressive athletes. Still, the circumstantial evidence is pretty convincing. Almost every day, newspapers are filled with stories of an ex-athlete and steroid user who is involved in some sort of fight or domestic violence.

Professional wrestler Chris Benoit killed his wife and son and then himself from what some believe was a result of 'roid rage.

One of the most famous cases involved professional wrestling star and steroid user Chris Benoit. On July 27, 2007, Benoit killed his wife and son. Two days later, he hung himself. Was Benoit's violent spree caused by a lifetime of steroid abuse? No one can say for sure. But one thing is certain: his autopsy revealed abnormally high amounts of testosterone in his blood.

In the end, there is no absolute proof that steroids lead every user to "roid rage." But the use

of anabolic steroids has been strongly linked to belligerent behavior. Gary Wadler, a doctor at New York University said, "I think a better way to view [steroid violence] is as a spectrum of behaviors by people on anabolic steroids, ranging from being somewhat more assertive, moving up one notch to being frankly aggressive, and moving up another notch to actually having this . . . rage."

Finally, stopping steroids almost always throws a user's hormones out of whack. Furthermore, the athlete's performance or appearance will suffer immensely. As a result and unless he or she keeps using the drugs, many steroid users become deeply depressed, especially when they discontinue the drug.

CHAPTER THREE

In Their Own Words

IT USUALLY BEGINS IN A GYM. SOMEONE suggests to a friend that he or she should try steroids. Coaches sometimes suggest it, too. Although the temptation to bulk up at any cost might be high, remember that steroid stories never end happily. What follows are the reports from users who were brave enough to come clean about the dark side of their experiences with gym candy.

Needle Nightmares

Most steroid users don't consider the health risks associated with injecting drugs. But shooting up often leads to painful side effects.

The first story is from an anonymous teenage wrestler who found that sticking a needle into his arm every day wasn't all he'd hoped for.

AT MY GYM, steroids were easy to get. I figured that they were no big deal, so I tried a cycle during my sophomore year wrestling season in high school. I bought a bottle of testosterone and a needle and syringe. I only wanted to have one syringe in my house because a bottle and a syringe are pretty easy to hide, but ten syringes would be pretty difficult, because I still live with my parents. Everyone told me that I needed to use a different needle every time I injected, but I thought I could just heat the needle up over a flame and it would be sterile. After a few weeks of shooting into my shoulder, it started to get swollen and looked weird. Then one day at wrestling practice, the place on my shoulder where I usually inject started to hurt and feel hot. My coach looked at it, and he thought it was badly infected, so we went to the hospital. When I was there, I had to tell the doctor how I got the infection, and my coach found out that I was using steroids, and he told my parents. I got suspended from school for a week and the wrestling team for the rest of the season, and all the kids in my school found out, too.

Val R. was a teenage bodybuilder who almost died from an injection she contracted from shooting up steroids.

I HAD AN infection in my shoulder and upper arm that looked like green, black, and yellow ink under my skin. The site was rock hard, and I got the worst case of strep throat I have ever had. . . . Even though I didn't do anything wrong during injection, sometimes stuff just happens. I guess I was unlucky. The dumbest thing I did was not going to a doctor. Although everything turned out all right, I could have lost my arm or worse. I could've died simply because I was too paranoid to ask for help.

32

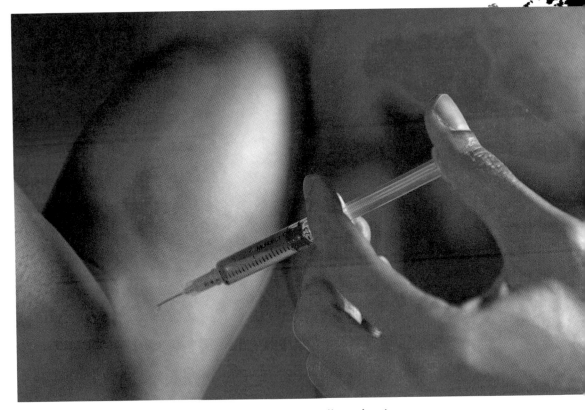

Many users inject steroids into their bodies using a needle and syringe. Reusing these needles can cause serious infection.

Steroids: Against the Law

As steroid use becomes more widespread, law enforcement is stepping up efforts to keep it under control. Though steroids are still entirely too easy to get, users beware: you might get yourself fined or arrested before you even have a chance to bulk up.

The first story is from a typical boy who wanted to take steroids to look a little bit better. Instead, he realized he was lucky he didn't end up in jail.

I WANTED TO look a bit better for the beach last year, so I researched anabolic steroids. I went online and found some place that offered to sell me steroids through the mail. I used a credit card and placed an order for some stuff that the site promised would help me lose some fat before the summer. I think it was about $500 worth of steroids. When the steroids arrived, I had to sign for them with the delivery person. As soon as I signed for them, I took them inside, and the doorbell rang again. It was the police. They said that I had signed for an illegal drug and pointed to the package that was still in my hands. Over the next few hours, they searched my house, my car, and my property. Eventually, they left, but they took the package with them. I think I was lucky because they didn't find anything in my house, and they didn't arrest me.

Illegal steroids can be purchased via the Internet.

But I never got to use the steroids I paid for and lost $500 that I really could have used for something else.

A One Way Ticket to the Trainer Table

Most steroid users assume that big muscles will naturally lead to better results on the ball field. But sports take more than brute strength. They also take agility and coordination. Of course, to participate, you have to be healthy. What follows is the confession of one student athlete who found himself singing the all too common song of steroid abuse: the "All Bulked Up But Riding the Bench" blues.

FOR ME, taking steroids was a natural move. I was an athlete in high school and got a college scholarship to play football at a major university. Between my senior year of high school and my freshman year of college, I started my first cycle because I thought I needed to be faster. I took injectable testosterone and Winstrol. I figured that Winstrol must be good because it's what Ben Johnson got busted using. I wanted to be fast like him. I was getting stronger at every workout and feeling great. I had heard that steroids can make your joints weaker, but I figured Ben Johnson didn't have that problem, so it was probably just a rumor. When the first day of training camp came up, my muscles were way too strong for my joints. I stopped using the steroids because I didn't want to hide them in my dorm room. I went into camp feeling strong, but . . .

my joints hurt and I couldn't keep up with the workouts. Eventually I got injured and missed most of my first season. Steroids just aren't worth the temporary boost.

Steroids and Aggression

Some steroid users say that 'roid rage is a myth. But most doctors see a definite correlation between steroid use and overly aggressive behavior.

The first quote is from a young man in the Midwest. He describes how steroids affected his buddies in the gym.

Steroids can bench an athlete due to joint weakness and injury.

ONE OF MY buddies did steroids (juice) for a year on and off. Before he started, he was a good kid everyone loved to be around. After, he beat . . . his girlfriend . . . ., beat up on everyone else smaller than him, and started in every illegal activity, from theft to scams.

I used to power-lift and bodybuild. About 85 percent of the pals at my gym used steroids. A long list of professional athletes and bodybuilders frequented the gym and got their stuff there. You could always find someone who had a bottle of testosterone or Winstrol.

Half the guys, and a few girls, went completely nuts. Always getting into fights and trouble with the law, when before using the junk, they were good, honest kids. Yep, kids—about 30 percent of the 'roid users were under twenty. Why? Because the "big guys" are doing it, and there's nothing wrong with it, especially if the pros are doing it.

The following story is from a weightlifter who discusses how steroids made him more violent.

WHILE USING steroids I couldn't stop getting into fights.

For all my life, pretty much, I have always felt mediocre in everything I do. In sports, the way I look, anything that has to do with

any kind of athletic venture. I started lifting weights at the age of sixteen. I was a flabby 170 pounds. At five feet six inches, nothing impressive at all, which really started getting to me . . . I started noticing the kids in my grade . . . were starting to get built and muscular, and it annoyed the [heck] out of me. No matter how much I worked out and ran, I was still behind everybody I knew.

After graduating school and still being a flabby mess . . . I started working at a gym near my house. The guys were . . . huge. Veins everywhere. . . . It was ridiculous. I remember talking to one of the guys there . . . and he told me all I ever wanted to know about anabolics. . . . I was sold. . . . By the fifth week my weight shot through the roof and my strength, too. I needed to get in shape for the summer, which was kind of hard, seeing that I was always breaking my hands on people's faces because I was constantly raging and getting in trouble, especially with the cops.

I remember getting into a fight raging at some guy who looked at me the wrong way, and his friend smashed a bottle over my face, permanently disfiguring my nose. I spent a night in jail.

Another thing: I was injecting close to my sciatic nerve, reusing needles and syringes, and not sanitizing the area. I got abscesses.

Here's the story of another user who found that steroid use led to problems with the law and random acts of violence.

I CAN'T COUNT how many fights I was in, but I do know I ended up needing reconstructive surgery on my hand. There were a lot of bad things that went along with my newfound body. I was going through girlfriends every other week (not so much a bad thing). I couldn't sit still for five minutes. I started smoking pot, I started fighting with my parents, (and) I even spent the night in jail. Not to mention the mental and physical side

effects that I encountered, some of which still currently plague me. Carpal tunnel syndrome, insomnia, depression, inconsistent sexual drive, criminal record, and the list could go on. These are very serious and most of the time are irreversible. . . . Steroids are just as powerful and just as dangerous as cocaine or crack . . . some of the mental side effects are just the same.

Steroids: No Long-term Side Effects? Guess Again

Sure, a little extra muscle can make a person seem more attractive. But how about an unnatural amount of extra muscle? Many people find it decidedly unattractive. Then there are the problems with acne and balding. The following steroid user found out the hard way how steroids can wreck a person's appearance for life.

I STARTED taking steroids in my early twenties to look better for girls. I was always kind of skinny and thought that I could go on a small cycle and get a bit bigger and be more attractive to women. I bought some pink pills from a guy at my gym. I think they were called "Diana-ball." I thought that was great, because I was trying to meet more girls, and "Diana" is a girl's name. At first I gained a lot of weight and strength. I thought I was looking better, but I still wasn't really meeting more girls. After a few weeks, I started noticing some hair falling out when I was in the shower. I didn't think about it at the time. I never had a problem with hair loss before. Before I knew it, my hairline started getting higher and the hair on the back of my head started getting thinner. I was going bald in my early twenties! I stopped using the little pink pills, but it didn't matter. The hair never really grew back, even after I stopped. I ended up losing hair and a lot of confidence when I was talking to women, all from using something that was supposed to help me meet more girls! I wish I never met "Diana."

Although steroid use can lead to permanent hair loss (and a host of other long-term health problems) in both

An unwelcome side effect of steroid use is loss of hair.

sexes, it can affect woman users uniquely. What follows is the statement of a female weight lifter, who lost a cherished gift as a result of steroid use.

I AM A twenty-one year old female and have been lifting weights in the gym since I was thirteen years old. I have always enjoyed working out with weights and just living a healthy lifestyle. Two years ago I started dating a bodybuilder who shared my passion for the gym and saw great potential in my genetics to compete in bodybuilding. He introduced me to hard training, healthy eating, and steroids.

Having never used any street drugs, little alcohol, and never smoking, I refused to have anything to do with steroids (not to mention I don't like needles). After much research and friendly persuasion from my boyfriend, I decided to try a cycle of Winstrol V and Primobolan. These steroids, according to him and others, were mild steroids popular among female bodybuilders. I was hesitant but convinced that these mild steroids weren't enough to harm me in any way and could only help.

During and after two cycles of these drugs I experienced mood changes, dramatic fat loss, increased lean body mass, and indescribable pumps in the gym. I didn't notice any negative side effects until . . . you see, I forgot to tell you that I was singer. My father sings, my mother sings, my sister has an annual concert, and my brother has a CD. Music is my life. Correction—*was* my life. A few months

after I finished the steroids I noticed my voice started cracking during conversation. The sound of my voice was inconsistent and unpredictable. I had to decline an invitation to sing at a friend's wedding, and I lost a singing contest because I couldn't reach any of the notes in the songs I usually competed with. I thought it was allergies (I suffer with those as well), but it wasn't.

It has been a year and a half, and my voice is deeper than it used to be. People who just meet me can't notice that there is anything wrong (I do not have a man's voice by any means). But my friends and family have noticed. What's more, they've noticed that I don't sing. I don't sing at family functions (a weekly event), and I politely decline all invitations to karaoke. I have been to throat doctors and voice centers. . . . The verdict: irreversible damage. The deepening of my voice is permanent, and in order to sing again I have to get voice lessons to retrain my voice to sing in an entirely different range than before.

Rob Garibaldi was an extremely talented baseball player. Despite a stellar high school record, pro scouts told him that he wasn't what they were looking for. It wasn't hard for Rob to figure out why: he was a boy with major-league talent but minor-league size. He needed to get bigger.

THE SAD STORY OF ROB GARIBALDI

Unfortunately, Rob turned to steroids. After he started, he found he couldn't stop. After a tumultuous six years of steroid abuse, Rob committed suicide at the age of twenty-four.

When Rob's father confronted him about his drug abuse shortly before his suicide, Rob shouted, "I'm on steroids. What do you think? Who do you think I am? I'm a baseball player. Baseball players take steroids. How do you think Bonds hits all his home runs? How do you think all these guys do all this stuff? You think they do it from just working out normally?"

As Rob's mother put it, "In his mind, he felt like all the guys were getting away with this. Cheating and doing this is part of what's going on every day, and it was required. . . . If Barry Bonds is doing it, Mark McGwire was doing it, then skinny little old him for sure had to be doing it."

Friends, family, and doctors noticed a huge difference in Rob's personality when he was on steroids. A psychiatrist he was seeing, said, "There was a really edgy, irritable quality when he was using steroids, like he was just ready to jump across the room and throttle you."

Though Rob eventually won a scholarship to the University of Southern California, one of the country's premier baseball programs, one of the fitness coaches told him that he needed to gain twenty more pounds. Using steroids already, Rob upped his dose even more. Though he had some moments of glory—in 2001 *Baseball America* named him one of the one hundred top college baseball players in the country—Rob's behavior become more and more erratic. His grades suffered. In June 2001, Rob was kicked off the team. After that, his life spiraled downward, until he ended it a little more than a year later. Rob's father saves much of his bitterness for Major League Baseball.

"I think it's sickening. I think the public looks at baseball players as back in the gladiator days. They are just to entertain, and if they want to screw themselves up, so what. But the problem is, no matter what anybody says, they are setting the bar for younger kids. And that bar is getting itself all the way down now to the junior high level."

I'm still in the gym and competing drug free in bodybuilding. But unfortunately I have lost something that I never fully understood was so important to me. The passion I had for singing and the deep-rooted love for music that is a part of my family history and pride will never be the same. I have made more improvements with my body in the past year with proper nutrition training and supplements, but the one decision I made two years ago haunts me every day of my life: when I talk, when I hear an old favorite song on the radio, when I listen to the melodic sound of my family singing, smiling, and longing for me to fill in a harmony heard only in my memories.

For every one of these stories, there are many more. Almost every school these days is full of kids who have used steroids. Don't let yourself be one of them!

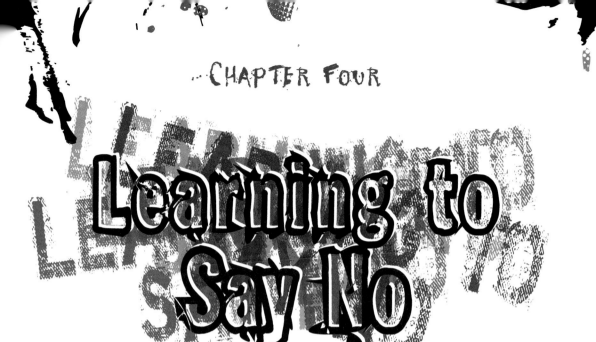

CHAPTER FOUR

Learning to Say No

SOMETIMES PRESSURES IN SCHOOL hallways and locker rooms make it hard to say no. But you can do it. There are ways to find the courage to let your friends know that you won't be using drugs.

How to Say No to Steroids

It can be tough to not go along with the crowd. Here are some easy strategies you can use to keep yourself away from performance-enhancing drugs.

- Sometimes the easiest solution is the most obvious. If you're in the weight room and someone is pushing you to try steroids, just say, "No thanks," and get back to your lifting. Be polite, but make it clear the conversation is over.

• If you're being pushed to try steroids, it can be helpful to have a fact or excuse ready. Say something like, "Sorry, man. I'm afraid of needles," or "I read about that stuff. It's deadly." You don't have to tell the other person not to take steroids. But you can make it clear with a single excuse that you just aren't interested.

A student athlete shows his support for saying "no" to steroid use.

• If someone is talking about steroids more than makes you comfortable, try changing the subject. One thing that works is to suggest doing something else. Say something like, "Hey, why don't we watch a video?" or "Let's go study for that test." Even if your friend doesn't want to join you, he or she will probably get the point that steroids aren't in your game plan.

• Sometimes it helps to be funny or flip. If people are bugging you about steroids, have some quick comebacks ready. Try out something like this:

"Nah. I don't want to turn into a giant, walking zit."

"Sorry, but my muscles are already too awesome to be believed. People might get jealous."

• If someone keeps bugging you, it can sometimes work to give them the cold shoulder. Just ignore everything he or she says. Turn your back to the person talking.

• If everyone you know who uses steroids works out at the gym together, plan your workouts for some other time. It's hard to pressure someone who isn't in the room.

• As the saying goes, there is strength in numbers. Hang out with the athletes in your school who are not using steroids. Be part of the clean crowd, and you'll stay clean yourself.

Remember, people respect others who have the courage of their convictions. In most cases, all you have to do

STEROID LINGO

Like almost any specialized activity, good or bad, steroid use has its own slang. Here is a list of some of the most commonly used words and expressions.

BLENDING the use of steroids with other drugs

DART, POKE, NED terms for syringes

FREAKY a term in bodybuilding to describe someone who is obviously on steroids

JUICE injectable steroids

PYRAMIDING when a user slowly escalates steroid use, then tapers it off

SHOTGUNNING taking steroids on an inconsistent basis

STACKING using steroids in combination

TEST testosterone

is say, "No." Just make sure you really mean it, and you might be surprised at how quickly the steroid users at your school leave you alone.

Using Steroids Is Cheating

Remind yourself and friends who are thinking of using performance-enhancing drugs that it is cheating. Steroids give the user an unfair and illegal advantage over the non-user—it's that simple. That makes steroid use no different than a pitcher throwing a spitball or a runner taking a shortcut. Yes, the world of sports is competitive. But there is no honor in winning by having an unfair advantage over an opponent. As clichéd as it may sound, the true satisfaction of winning comes from playing by the rules. Basketball great Michael Jordan put it correctly when he said that it wasn't losing that he feared, just "not trying." Take it from Mike. Most important in any sport is to practice hard, play hard, and play fairly.

Cheating by taking anabolic steroids is even worse than rigging a race or corking a bat—that's because performance-enhancing drugs are so dangerous. When enough people in a sport are using anabolic steroids, it puts pressure on *everybody* to use in order to stay competitive.

When one athlete uses steroids, he or she has an unfair advantage creating an unbalanced playing field.

For instance, there are those who believe that Barry Bonds, who stands accused of taking steroids, did it only after he saw Mark McGwire and Sammy Sosa start bashing all of those home runs. By 1998 Barry Bonds had won three Most Valuable Player Awards. A complete player, Bonds could hit, throw, and steal bases. Even so, with McGwire and Sosa suddenly killing the ball, some sportswriters guess that Bonds turned to drugs so he could hit more home runs, too.

The same thinking that may have influenced Bonds to take performance-enhancing drugs influences student athletes all across the world. Most likely, many current steroid users once had no interest in taking drugs. But when faced with the perception that everyone else is doing it, they felt as though they had no choice.

54

How to Tell When Your Best Friend Is on Steroids

Many steroid users keep it to themselves, anticipating what others will say: "It's unhealthy." "It can be addictive." "It's cheating." Unlike some other drug users, steroid abusers can be easy to spot. Here is a list of warning signs to look out for around school and the locker room.

- Sudden weight gain and unusually large muscles. Unfortunately, anabolic steroids work. Most users will gain weight and put on muscle. If the ninety-pound freshman returns to school as a sophomore sporting biceps as big as volleyballs, it's pretty likely that he is on the juice.
- Obsessiveness with working out and weight lifting. Anabolic steroids work best when coupled with intense weight lifting. Most people who take steroids get pretty obsessed with their bodies. Other, more common interests, get swallowed up by repeated workouts, reading fitness magazines, and staring in the mirror.

One sign of steroid use is an obsession with heavy weight lifing.

• Sudden flare-up of acne, especially on the back and neck. The side effect that is impossible to avoid is one of the most noticeable. Of course, many teenagers suffer from bad skin already. But most teens get their pimples on their face, not on their back. And the blemishes associated with steroid use are usually bigger and more painful looking than those encountered by the typical nonusing adolescent.

• Irritable behavior. Again, most teenagers are irritable at times. It's part of growing up. But being occasionally irritable is one thing—irritation that turns the corner to outright

aggressive or violent behavior is another. If someone you know is suddenly prone to aggressive outbursts, he or she might be on steroids.

If anyone you know exhibits some or all of these warning signs, don't look away. Are you close friends with the person you think is using steroids? Maybe you can take him or her aside and confess your concern. If that doesn't

CHANGING THE MYTH

One way to get kids to stop using steroids is through a dose of hard-nosed reality. Many student athletes use steroids because they think it will help them get to the pros. Nothing could be further from the truth. For most people, focusing one's energies on playing professional sports is like training for a career that doesn't exist. Statistically, it is next to impossible to make it as a pro athlete. Unfortunately, there are some coaches and parents who push the idea of a pro career so hard that they pressure students into doing whatever they can to succeed. Don't forget: organized sports are a great way to make friends and learn to be part of a team. Above all, sports are a way to have fun. Almost no one gets paid for playing sports. Is it really worth ruining your long-term health for a goal that's virtually unattainable?

work (or if the user is someone you can't approach), talk to a coach, teacher, or parent. People on steroids need help. Help someone get clean before the damage to his or her health is too severe.

Get Help

Many doctors feel that anabolic steroids can be addictive as users get hooked on the rush of all that testosterone coursing through their bodies and the sight of all those new muscles. But with a little help, a steroid user can get clean. The main thing is not to be scared to ask for help. If your coach is pushing you to take some illegal supplements, tell your parents. If your parents won't help, go to a friend or a teacher, anyone you can trust.

Today, health and school officials are much more aware of the steroid problem. Most schools will have someone on staff who can point a user to a doctor, a therapist, or some sort of treatment program. If you are already on steroids and want to stop, do it under a doctor's supervision. It's not good to have anabolic steroids in your body, but after starting, it is important to stop gradually. Quitting cold turkey can throw a user's natural hormones out of whack and lead to a severe depression.

Glossary

adolescence the teenage years

anabolic steroids the type of steroids associated with rapid weight gain and muscle growth

athletic supplements health and vitamin drinks and powders taken by athletes to gain strength, sometimes laced with illegal steroids

cardiovascular system pertaining to the body's heart, lungs, veins, and arteries

cysts closed sacs formed in animal tissues, containing fluid or semifluid matter

epiphyseal plates plates in children and adolescents located on each end of the body's long bones that remain open, permitting growth, and then fuse at adulthood

gangrene a potentially life-threatening condition when a mass of body tissue dies

psychiatric pertaining to the mind and emotional difficulties

testosterone the hormone used in most anabolic steroids

Find Out More

BOOKS

Beamish, Rob. *Steroids: A New Look at Performance Enhancing Drugs*. New York: Praeger, 2011.

Kiesbye, Stefan. *Steroids*. Farmington Hills, MI: Greenhaven Press, 2008.

Knight, Erin. *Steroids*. New York: Crabtree Publications, 2011.

Marshall Cavendish Reference. *Drugs of Abuse*. New York: Marshall Cavendish, 2012.

Marshall Cavendish Reference. *Substance Abuse, Addiction, and Treatment*. New York: Marshall Cavendish, 2012.

DVD

Steroid Abuse: Win Now, Lose Later. Educational Video Network, 2006.

WEBSITES

Kids Health: Steroids

http://kidshealth.org/parent/emotions/behavior/steroids.html
    A website geared for children and their parents on the
    dangers of steroid abuse.

The Mayo Clinic: Steroids: Know the Risks

www.mayoclinic.com/health/performance-enhancing-
    drugs/HQ01105
One of the most prominent hospitals in the world
    devotes a page to steroids and their risks.

The National Institute on Drug Abuse

http://teens.drugabuse.gov/facts/facts_ster1.php
    A website devoted to assessing the health risks
    associated with using anabolic steroids.

Index

Pages in **boldface** are illustrations

About the Author

DANIEL BENJAMIN is the author of several nonfiction works for young readers, including books on green cars and extreme sports. He lives in New York City with his wife and two children.